A Woman of Aran

The Life and Times of Bridget Dirrane

As told to Rose O'Connor and Jack Mahon

BLACKWATER PRESS

Acknowledgements

Editor	Anna O'Donovan
Layout & Design	Paddy Barrett
ISBN	0 86121 962 7

The authors and publishers would like to thank Marie Mannion and the staff of Galway Family History Society West for initial editing and typing up of script.

British Library Cataloguing-in Publication Data.

A catalogue record for this book is available from The British Library.

Produced in Ireland by:

Blackwater Press

c/o Folens Publishers

8 Broomhill Business Park

Tallaght

Dublin 24.

Table of Contents

Introduction

'Aran my home', Bridget describes it as rugged, sandy, stony yet fertile and green. Bridget Gillan Dirrane now 103 years of age, has finally found the opportunity to tell her story, to commit to paper a myriad of experiences that have coloured a remarkable life.

As Matron of St Francis' Home in Newcastle, Galway where Bridget now resides, Bridget used to recount these wonderful stories to me. Bridget's stories were so interesting that I decided to record them all.

An avid Gaeilgeoir and musician, Bridget has been blessed with good health all her life. Her memory is remarkable and lucid; her speech is clear; she is very dignified, yet appreciates the simple things of life. Bridget has good days and bad days but no matter what day, there is always a twinkle in her shy, blue eyes. She married twice and although wasn't blessed with children of her own, she spent many enjoyable years nursing, caring and rearing children. Her pride and joy are her three step-grandchildren in Cliff Edge Cottage, Timmy, Michael and Ciarán, to whom she dedicates this book.

As Matron I felt this story needed to be recorded and passed on so I contacted Blackwater Press Publishers and through the good offices of John O'Connor and Anna O'Donovan, interested them in the idea, the end result being the publication of *A Woman of Aran*. For me this has been a labour of love. Blackwater Press prevailed on their well-known author Jack Mahon who had four previous books of his published by them to do the writing. Jack visited St Francis' Home almost every day, developing this, checking out that and, armed with his tape recorder, got Bridget to develop certain stories.

I, too, became enthralled with Bridget's story and looked forward to my every visit. I was always greeted with a smile from Bridget herself and everything was made easy for me by Matron Rose and, indeed, all the staff at the home. Finally, I'd like to thank my good friends Florrie and Paddy Barrett for their usual courtesy and efficiency in the design and setting of the book.

We hope you, the readers, get as much enjoyment out of reading the book as we have done compiling it. It is a simple book, full of love and adventure, recalling the life and times of a fantastic woman who still cherishes life at 103 and, who considers every day a bonus. It has been an honour, a pleasure and an education to have had the opportunity to share in the telling of such a wonderful story.

Jack Mahon

Sitting in her room in St Francis' Home Bridget sends this message to the people of Aran: 'Always be kind to your neighbours and your neighbour will look after you. Love the islands and treat them with respect. Be proud of where you live and enjoy the clean fresh air that God gave equally to all.'

November, 1997

Dedicated to my step-grandchildren,
Timmy, Michael and Ciarán

Chapter 1

Thanks be to God and His Blessed Mother

It was always my ambition to erect a statue of thanksgiving to Our Blessed Lady on the Aran I love for all she had done for me during my life. Our Lady has brought me safely through many crises, not least when I was a young eight-year-old girl on Inishmore, the largest of the three Aran islands, when I developed a very severe abscess on my neck of which I still bear a scar at the age of 103. That abscess grew and grew and seemed to get bigger and longer daily. My parents, *go ndéana Dia trócaire orthu* (God rest them both), were at their wits end as to what to do with me. If a doctor was mentioned I ran a mile away for fear of having the abscess lanced.

It came as a result of measles, not seen before by my parents. I was in desperate pain and couldn't open my mouth. An old woman named Celia Mullins lived in Gort na gCapall. Though not a native of Aran, she was much respected for her healing powers and sometimes, peculiar ways. My mother asked her to see me when the pain was at its worst. Her advice was to poultice the abscess with a mixture of sugar, butter and potato. However, it was all to no avail.

One day, around this time, my mother was combing my long, flowing hair which came down to my waist. As sometimes happens the comb caught in a little tangle of hair, slipped and hit the abscess. As you might imagine, I screamed and screamed. My father was present, he got agitated and a slight disagreement broke out between them. This was very unusual as they seldom disagreed and I remember him clearly saying to 'leave the child alone'. With that, my mother grabbed her shawl and left the house. I watched her head towards the well where the statue of Our Lady is now erected. There are three wells in the vicinity, one a holy well.

My mother took a sea-shell with her which she filled with holy water from the well in Corough. On her way back she met Celia Mullins who sent her back to collect ivy leaves from the well. She advised her to mix some earth with the water and ivy and apply it as a poultice to my neck. Believe me that did the trick. Early next morning I woke up soaking wet and wakened my sister Julia, who slept beside me, to show her all the pus and badness that had seeped out. It ran for some time afterwards but eventually dried up. In the end, a snail was put on my neck to dry it up completely. It did the work of a leech and the wound healed up in time.

I remember going back to the well myself often to thank God and His Blessed Mother for curing me. This event left a marked impression on me all through life. After that my mother often strayed off to the holy well and got great peace of mind there. Many people received cures at it. Crowds come there now especially on Lady's Day, August 15, when rosaries are said. The people of Aran know well that Our Lady has bestowed many blessings on them down through generations.

I didn't know how best to thank Her and God for all the blessings He and Our Lady have bestowed on us and all the healing we received no matter what illness, upset or accident befell us. One day Coleman Dirrane, my son-in-law and myself decided it was time to pay Our Lady back. We went to Galway; I took whatever money I had with us and bought a statue that would be a permanent and fitting memorial to her. The specially-ordered stone statue, painted by myself is designed to withstand the elements and cost £500.

It was blessed at a special ceremony on the site of the holy well in Corough in 1994. I was 100 years old then. Coleman was a great help in organising it all. A rosary was said by An t-Athair Ó Dubhshláine, Fr Mannion and Fr Dara Molloy before a huge gathering of Aran people. The statue is erected at the Well Of The Four Beauties as it is known. According to legend, four beautiful saints are buried beneath the statue.

I was there that day and was so happy to have the statue erected, something I had wished to do for so long. It had been a long life. I'd like Pat Waters (Pádraig Ó Tuairisg) to build a solid bridge at the site to prevent accidents. He is a man for whom I have great respect and I pray for him daily. Fr Dara Molloy is another true friend, a great preacher. God will take care of them all.

Last September, I travelled by plane to Aran. Hopefully it won't be my last visit. I thank God for bringing me safely there. Not bad for one at 103! My right foot isn't too good at present. This statue is going to be in Aran after me and I've donated it to the people of Aran, my native place and the place I love. My hope is that the people of Aran will maintain it and build a proper walk to it. Long after I'm forgotten I hope they will revere it and hope they keep it painted as it is now because if the paint goes, the statue becomes a colourless piece of stone.

Sometimes it may take 100 years to get a thing done right but it's better done late than never. There are still things I have to do today and a lot more tomorrow. I always loved Our Lady and so did my father and mother. In our house my parents had a big statue of Our Lady on a stand in the corner of their bedroom. The main statue was surrounded by some smaller ones. One time my mother was sick in bed and when visiting her I reached up and knocked one of the smaller statues over and broke it. My mother cried over that. That's another reason why I'm so glad to have erected the memorial to Our Lady in Corough. You should all go and visit it some day.

Chapter 2

My First Day at School in Oatquarter

It is all of 100 years since I first went to school at Oatquarter National School but I remember it clearly as if it was yesterday. I was born Bridget Gillan on November 15, 1894, the youngest and smallest of eight children to Joseph and Margaret (nee Walsh) in the townland of Oatquarter, Inishmore. My parents were married in St Ann's Church in Oughill on April 17, 1876. My father was 23 years of age and my mother a mere 19-year-old. Pat, the eldest, was born on March 8, 1879. After him came Mary, Julia, Joseph, John, George and Margaret Anne. I can still rattle off the birthdays of each one of them. They are all long since gone of course, *go ndéana Dia trócaire orthu* (God rest them both).

I remember well my first day at school. Being the youngest and the last of the clan to go to school I was, of course, spoilt rotten. The school was close by. Pat, my eldest brother (and my favourite), took me there that first day. As a young flier of three, I was carried on his broad shoulders until we reached the front gate of the school. My first impression was that the school looked huge. I was put sitting on a stool beside my two brothers John and George who were assigned by the teachers, Mrs Callinan and Mrs O'Callaghan, both from County Clare, to take care of me. I wore a lovely pair of patent black shoes that first day, which had been purchased in England by a cousin of mine.

Mrs O'Callaghan gave me a slate and my wonders were at its solidity and whether it would be easy to break. The day passed quickly. It wasn't that strange because Margaret Anne was also there. Pat and the others had left to start work. Pat worked as a fisherman. But my old favourite Pat was back from his fishing to collect me at the end of the day and hoist me home on his back once again. We met my uncle George *ar ár mbealach abhaile* (on our way home) and I can still hear him saying, 'Come here my own little darling, and tell me, what did Mrs O'Callaghan teach you today?' He was another great favourite of mine.

Chapter 3

Other school memories of Aran

We were mixed in the baby classes (*na naíonáin*) and school finished earlier for the very junior classes. As we got older we were divided into boys' and girls' classes. National School finished at fourth class then. It was, in many ways, much the same as it is today.

Irish was our native tongue. We had it from the *cliabhán* (the cradle) so to speak; we spoke English in our house too. Both my father and mother could speak English which was unusual. We were encouraged to speak and learn English at school so that we could get on well, when, and if, we left Aran. *Tá neart Gaeilge agam fós* (I still have plenty of Irish). It was always my favourite language and I often spoke Irish in

Boston afterwards. Even today Irish comes very natural to me.

After we left the *naíonáin* there were 15 girls in my class. I remember Nora Fleming, Barbara Conneely, Bridget Mullen, Anne Flaherty, Nora Connelly, Catherine and Delia Mullen and Catherine Dirrane. We all got on well.

The school I went to is now the site of a home on the island. The new schoolhouse is the third national school in Oatquarter in my time. My three step-grandchildren, Timmy, Michael and Ciarán (to whom this book is dedicated) are now students in the Oatquarter National School. When we started school, we were given lead pencils and slates. Later on we graduated to pen and paper. The ink was in inkwells in the desks. We sat about five or six to a desk.

I didn't like school that much. Our only source of heat was from a turf fire. Everyone of us brought a sod of turf to school each day and that sufficed. An inspector called to the school once a year and each child was separately examined. He was a strict man. It was an exciting time for the school and we didn't rest easy until we saw him saying goodbye and leaving.

Prayers and Catechism were very much part of the curriculum. I was often slapped at school and I wouldn't like when Margaret brought the *scéal* (story) home with her because that meant another slap from Mammy as I wouldn't admit to doing anything wrong.

As I look back it was mostly happy memories but my whole world collapsed when my eldest and favourite brother, Pat, died shortly after I started school. He was the lad who carried me to school that first day. My heart was broken. After he died, I expected every boat coming in from the ocean to have Pat on it. I was sure he'd come back alive. Pat died of pneumonia for which there was no cure at the time.

Geography and English were two of my favourite subjects. One day I got lost in school and the whole student body was sent looking for me. Eventually, I was found in the turf-shed fast asleep!

I remember well my First Communion Day. That was a very special day and the priest who administered the sacrament was our Parish Priest, Father Murty Farragher. I wore a white medium dress with a long, white veil. My mother bought it specially for me at Frank McDonagh's in Galway. It was worn for Sunday Mass many times after that.

Another school memory is of going to Galway with my cousin, Bridget Walsh, and my sister Margaret Anne and the other school girls in our school singing group. We sang on the stage of the Town Hall and stayed in a hotel close to Eyre Square. I was only eight then and we travelled to Galway by boat, either the *Durass* or the *Dun Aengus*. It wasn't my first time visiting Galway. Seeing Galway for the first time was a great experience. There were plenty of small houses in Galway then. I remember buying a bag of grapes in a small shop. After getting to the hotel I found one of the grapes was rotten. I returned to the shop and had it replaced! So even at the tender age of eight I was nobody's fool.

One final story of schooldays. When I was in fourth or final class, I remember teaching *na naíonáin* their prayers and catechism and headlines such as the alphabet. It was the mode of the time. At holiday time I organised the choir when the teachers went home to County Clare on holidays or at Christmas and Easter in our parish church at Oughill. One of the lads called me 'teacher' from then on. His name was Willie Mullen. Years afterwards we met often in Boston at social functions. Willie was from Ballinacregga and ever afterwards when he saw me he always teased me with the salutation, 'Here comes the teacher.'

I left school at the age of 14.

Chapter 4

Mammy and Daddy and the Weaving tradition

My mother died of pneumonia after getting a cold. She worked right up to the end and was, at that stage, looking after her grandchildren. She was in her seventies. I have great memories of her. I wasn't her pet; Margaret Anne, the girl next to me was her real pet. We all loved Mammy. She wore herself to the bone to get things for all of us. She made all our clothes, knitted, and was accomplished at sewing. She washed, scrubbed and prepared the meals for all and sundry. The kettle was put on for any visitor. Ours, if you like, was a *flaithiúl* (generous) house. You see my father was a weaver and next door, my uncle George was also a weaver. There were many callers to both houses.

The Gillans inherited the weaving tradition on Inishmore. The weaver did the main work but he needed somebody else to wind up the bobbins of the yarn so as to make the flannel. I often wound the bobbins myself. The tradition of weaving and the Gillans came from way, way back, from *ghlún to glún* (generation to generation) so to speak.

The yarn had to be warped first. Then it had to be fitted into the loom. And so he worked away to make the flannel. That flannel clothed everyone on the island. People used to come and place orders for flannel. The Gillans were really the weavers of the island. My father was a small farmer as well. He grew his own vegetables in our own garden. There was no scarcity of food. My father was a very kind man and I never remember him slapping any of us. He didn't like to see Mammy slapping us either. They got on like a house on fire.

Prayer was very important in our house. The rosary was said every morning. My uncle George knelt every day at 12 o'clock, hail rain or shine and said the rosary next door. It was said in our house again at night and if we had any visitors they had to say a decade. It was always *tré Gaeilge* (in Irish) but my mother said the litanies in English. The trimmings, as we used to call them, were often as long as the rosary and they used to get my cousin, Pat Flaherty, down. I remember him once saying to Mammy: 'Maggie, when you're saying the rosary the next night, don't spend the whole night talking to the saints!'

We had two dogs in our house in our young days, Nelson and Bruno. I loved both of them. My mother wore this long pleated skirt and when she sat down at the fire to knit, one of the dogs always sat on her skirt on the floor beside her. And he lay there at her feet until she moved to get up. My mother always wore a shawl when going out. It was the style of the time. On Sundays and special days she wore a good brown one. For everyday use she wore a simple black one. I wore one myself at the age of 16 but I never liked the shawl and got rid of it as soon as I could!

My father predeceased my mother, dying at the young age of 62. Actually my father's death is much fainter in memory than the earlier death of my brother, Pat. The latter I'll never forget. I was only about eight when Daddy died. It is possible I was sent elsewhere in the island for his funeral.

I used to follow my mother everywhere. Often down to the shore where they used to gather seaweed, spread it out on the rocks to dry and then stack it when dry to make kelp. Even after she slapped me, I never let her out of the house by herself. We often went to the well for water together. Once, when I had left the island, she stumbled and fell passing through a stile into a local shop. While being attended to she said: 'This wouldn't have happened me if my Bridget was home'. I was sad when she died. My mother and father are buried in Killeany with my brother Pat along with the rest of the Gillans. My second husband Pat Dirrane is buried there too. And I'll be buried there too alongside them all. I would not go anywhere else.

Chapter 5

Ancient Cures of Aran

Cure, cure, kill or cure,
Doctors differ and patients die.

S o goes the jingle. I don't think we will ever see the day when all mankind will be free of sickness or disease. Human nature will always take its own course and not too many will survive to be 100! In days gone by people believed in the cures handed down from generation to generation. So it was in the Aran of my youth.

One of my memories centres on seeing my mother taking care of George, my brother, who had contracted pneumonia. She placed some empty tumbler glasses, up to four, open side down on his chest. This continued two or three times a day for seven or eight days. The idea was that the suction process would help the lungs to open up a bit and relieve the symptoms. The glasses would be left on the chest for a few minutes. Strangely enough she did cure George then and also many of our neighbours who complained of the same disease. In those days, you must remember, it wasn't unusual to hear of a person being sick today and dead on the morrow. Iodine was much used too and often a patient's chest was completely painted with iodine. It provided a help to warm the lungs and was used widely too for cuts and bruises.

For measles the best cures of all were the herbs. Mammy used to pick the wild nettles, boil and strain them to create a juice which was most effective once the spots appeared on the skin. This juice was given to neighbours in need too. For bad coughs the mullen plant was best of all. It has a long broad leaf and grows like nettles on the side of the road. Again, a juice was made of it after boiling, cooking and straining. Some people added sugar to the mixture which was taken either hot or cold.

For cuts, a plant called *slánlus*, in English, ribwort plantain, was extremely effective. The leaf has a smooth and a rough side and the rough side was put next to the cut or ulcer. It would stay on the cut until it was healed and would then fall off. Of course, you needed a bandage to keep it in place. I remember splitting my index finger while opening a tin of sardines in Aran and the *slánlus* did the job for me in seven days. Cobwebs were often used in the old days too to stop bleeding. There was no scarcity of cobwebs at the time but that particular usage is largely a thing of the past.

Carron oil was a concoction widely used for burns. This was made by dipping a red-hot piece of limestone rock in cold water. When allowed to cool, the water minus whatever scum had gathered at the top was mixed with linseed oil and beaten with a mixer to create a yellow cream. This cream rubbed on the burn and then bandaged up was generally very soothing and effective. Carron oil was also used for scalds. Horehound, another plant which grew on the side of the road, was used in times of loss of blood or of blood disorders. As with nettles and *slánlus*, the potion was created by the same boiling process. I remember a girl in Aran who had weak blood and was very run down being given this prescription by my mother and she was better in no time at all.

For a thorn stab or to remove a thorn, raw bacon was put over the sore area and if applied by means of a bandage for a few days, the flesh became soft and the thorn would slip out with a little pressure. Porter was used as a tonic for nursing mothers. It gave nourishment to mother and baby and when times were hard it was the only tonic available. *Poitín* (poteen) was regarded as a pain-killer and was also used to get rid of a cold if one got the shivers.

For mild burns, a paste of bread soda was a sure remedy. For nettle stings, dock leaves were the answer. Some of these cures persist to this day. In cases of bad nosebleeds, pieces of cold steel or silver were placed at the base of the neck and this would help to stem the flow. The cure for warts, corns and chilblains was the raw potato. We used to slice it, then rub it directly on and around the affected areas. The acid in the potato was the great healing factor. I remember curing a friend of mine from Glenina Heights in Galway who had a dose of warts on her hand by recommending the raw potato process to her.

Another herbal cure was the *macánleonta* (fennel). This was scraped off the plant and created a very sticky paste. One American visitor who fell in the graveyard, while visiting the grave of his ancestors, hurt his elbow and shoulder greatly. I applied the *macánleonta* sticky paste and when he got to Galway and was X-rayed, he was told the Aran remedy couldn't be bettered.

Dr Keane was the doctor on the island in my early youth. Dr Keane was a very kind and intelligent man. I remember also a Dr O'Brien from County Clare who came after him. He actually employed me to look after his grandchild in his house in Kilronan. The doctor lived a good distance away from most island people and anyone who was sick had to be transported by horse and cart. If the illness was serious the doctor would be sent for.

Chapter 6

Drownings generated Great Commotion in Aran

I spent many happy hours in the church at Oughill. I used to accompany my family to Sunday Mass. We walked to the church, which was a short mile from our house but other residents of the island had a longer distance to travel. There was a second church St Brigid's in Kilronan but St Ann's in Oughill was our church. There is a third church at the other end of the island now.

Sunday was a very holy day in Aran and the Mass was the big occasion of the week. All the women wore their best shawls and the men their best waistcoats. Mass started at 11 a.m. and it would be close to one o'clock before it finished. Sometimes we'd have breakfast before Mass but if we were fasting to receive Holy Communion, no food was consumed until after one o'clock.

We went to Mass in little groups. My father and mother would walk together. The lads were in groups of two or three and similarly with the girls in our family. We'd join some of our cousins who lived next door. We usually sat in the same seat but if that was gone we sat or knelt elsewhere. People mostly knelt. Very few people in the island ever missed Sunday Mass. Unless you were very sick you were always there. Mass was, of course, in Latin then and the sermons were delivered partly through Irish and partly through English. The Rosary was recited *trí Ghaeilge ar fad*. I often heard my father speak with affection of how in the days of yore all the Gillan family would gather together in the house after Mass, where they'd be given food and drink. They were known at the time as the Gillan Congregation.

The priests I remember best from those early days were the PP Fr Murty Farragher and Fr Owens. The Parish Priest was a very important man in the community. He did everything for the Aran Island people. He was almost like a parent. He helped to organise the fishing tackle and arranged to get nets for those who had none and often lent a shilling or two to those in need. There was great respect for the priest then. The local men always doffed their hats and bent their knees when they saw him coming and the women always bowed their heads and curtsied. All those respectful habits are gone now although there are a few left who have not forgotten.

Wakes lasting all night, sometimes longer, followed all deaths on the island. People walked miles to attend a funeral. Your absence would be missed. The only conversation concerned the corpse laid out in front of you. A lot of young people died in those days and the young deaths caused great heartbreak. The parents would be crestfallen. Drink, especially the home-made brew, was very much part of the scene. There was tobacco for men and tea and bread for the ladies. The tobacco was available in a round coil from which you could chop off as much as you required. Often the older women could be heard crying all night. This *caoineadh* (crying or keening) could be heard for miles around and was very eerie. I remember the wake of my very first teacher, Bridget Callaghan (died July 30, 1910). That wake lasted for two days and two nights. She was an old lady and was very well liked in the area. She is buried in Kilmurvey graveyard.

Drownings in Aran generated awful commotion and anxiety on the island though it was a very rare occurrence, thankfully. I remember one particular drowning accident vividly. James O'Flaherty and Mr Flanagan, a schoolteacher had travelled by currach to visit a Holy Well somewhere in Connemara. That same day Laurence Connolly from Onaght, who had been married two months previously, walked to Kilronan to have his marriage registered. While there he met the men who had gone to the Holy Well and another Tom Dirrane who offered to give him a lift home to Onaght in their currach. On their way back, all four—O'Flaherty, Flanagan, Dirrane and Connolly—were drowned when a huge wave struck the boat. The island mourned that tragedy for months afterwards. Laurence Connolly's heartbroken young wife remained on the island for some time but eventually emigrated, like so many others, to Boston. Other drowning tragedies saw the drowning of my own cousin Michael O'Flaherty whose boat was struck by a wave while out fishing in Galway Bay. Martin Dillane from Kilronan was also drowned while Anthony O'Flaherty lost his life when his currach was wrecked between Kilronan and Connemara.

We always looked forward to Easter Sunday and Christmas Day. The people of Aran always fasted on Holy Saturday in preparation for Easter Sunday. Some of the older folk had the habit of eating too many eggs on Good Friday! The meat on Easter Sunday in the form of a goose, a duck, a hen or a piece of bacon or beef brought specially from Galway, was eagerly awaited. Easter Sunday was a great day with Benediction after Mass. I had a good singing voice then and, as I mentioned before, looked after the choir in the absence of the teachers at holiday time. The Benediction hymns included the Latin hymns *Tantum Ergo* and the *O Salutaris*.

Christmas was another great time. The weather was usually severe and trips to Galway were limited. I remember we had plenty of currant and raisin cakes and the meal, like at Easter, centred around geese, ducks or hens which were plentiful on Aran. Santa Claus came to Aran too with pairs of shoes or clothing but he always seemed to come down the chimney and go away without any of us seeing him!

At that time, apart from candles and oil lamps, there was no light in the church. There was no heat at all. We never carried lights when out walking at night. We got used to making our way in the dark. In our house a little kerosene lamp used to be lit right next to our door inside near the window. We used to see that little light shining through the window as we came up the low road and it led us home.

Chapter 7

Making Tea and Sandwiches for Pearse

When you're a centenarian plus like me it is difficult to look back on it all and remember everything clearly. As I approach 103 I have good days and bad days and I hope I live to see the launch of this book *le cúnamh Dé* (with the help of God). Even though my mind hops all over the place, I can remember many things clearly as if they happened yesterday.

Music was very much part of our young lives. Michael Wallace my cousin, who could play both the accordion and fiddle, was my music teacher. Dancing was popular too and we learnt to dance sets, hornpipes and barn dances. Margaret, my sister, was a fine fiddle player and brother Joe played the accordion. So music was very much part of our house and to round it off my mother played the jew's harp. Michael Wallace often played in our house until after midnight. (Incidentally, I'm also related to the well-known Irish musician Joe Dirrane, now in the USA). George my brother, who later became a Schools Inspector of Irish was known in our house as 'the college man'. George was trained in Tourmakeady, County Mayo along with Sinéad Flanagan who later married Éamon de Valera and they were firm friends through life. Tourmakeady was a big college then and George did his best to persuade me to go there. However, nursing, tending and caring for people was in my blood. I was well versed in many of the Aran cures and I always wanted to be a nurse. Anyway one needed lots of money to be trained as a teacher in Tourmakeady. Everything you wore and everything you used had to be made in Ireland. Any money that came my mother's way went towards George's education. He came back to teach Irish in Tourmakeady before taking up the position of School's Inspector.

We had many famous visitors to Inishmore. At one time I was staying in the Concannon home in Onaght as a companion to a five-year-old Concannon boy. I spent a year looking after him before he went to school. Very important visitors to the Concannon house included Pádraig Pearse (1879-1916) leader of the Easter Rising who was executed May 3, 1916, Thomas Ashe, a volunteer (died Mountjoy Jail September 17, 1917), Éamonn Ceannt (a signatory of the 1916 Proclamation) and Joseph Mary Plunkett (volunteer

1887–1916). These men who regularly visited Aran stayed in St Ronan's in Kilronan. I remember well making tea for these four men during the month of August, one of the years before 1916.

We knew they were involved in the volunteers but were told to keep our mouths closed and not to broadcast anything we heard. They were four ordinary young fellows, nothing extraordinary about them.

Even then I was nationally minded myself and this, of course, came from my home. Martin Concannon went to the US as a young man, returned and built a home in Onaght. He was a wonderful Irishman and these men who were all teachers often came to visit him. I was still in Aran when the Rising took place in 1916. I felt quite sad that so many people lost their lives and some of these included the men I had made tea and sandwiches for in Concannon's. I had overheard them talking about the Rising, and, being a slip of a girl and thinking I had no English, they took no notice of me. But yet I never told anybody about what I had heard. I kept the *béal dúnta* (mouth closed) and never breathed a word to anybody.

We had other famous visitors then also. There was Austin Stack (Irish delegation to Lloyd George 1921) and Thomas McDonagh (executed with Pádraig Pearse in 1916). It saddens me to this day that all those good men were so cruelly executed. Thomas McDonagh's wife gave me a velvet hat and coat which I wore for years afterwards.

The day to leave Aran was fast approaching.

Chapter 8

Leaving Aran for the First Time for Tuam

I was now in my late teens and, of course, had been to
Galway by boat a number of times. So I had no fear of
leaving the island. My last job on the island was working
in a big store in Kilmurvey which had a fish-curing station.
Anyone who was able to open, clean and wash fish was
employed. A big ship was anchored out in the bay and the
fish were shipped out to it. It was a good time for Aran, with
so many getting employment.

Some other memories of Aran surface now as I reminisce
on my first departure from it. As children, we loved going to
the beach which we called Portcorough, a small port which
lies near Polsheela. My mother used to warn us not to swim
in Aran because of the rocks and stringy seaweed and we did

what she told us. In those days your parents' word was law. Boats laden with turf came from Connemara to this port. Later on, the boats came to Port Murvey when the pier was developed there. These boats also carried seaweed. Many a time the eight of us would work together, heaping up the seaweed on creels and take it to the land to fertilise the soil. We often brought 20 loads of seaweed per day. Our donkey was a real beauty and we called him 'Blackbird'. He could nearly talk to you!

We didn't have a boat of our own as they were too expensive and difficult to maintain. But there were plenty of boats on the island and we could go to Galway whenever we needed to. I was never afraid to travel anywhere by boat even though I couldn't swim. Fish and potatoes were always very plentiful in Aran and food was never scarce. Every family in Aran killed their own sheep. They kept their own ducks and hens who kept them supplied with eggs. There were plenty of rabbits there too. All these foods provided the necessary ingredients for a healthy life.

For a time in Aran I worked for Dr O'Brien in Kilronan, looking after his grandchild and this acquaintance led ultimately to my first job outside Aran. At first, he used to collect me and take me to his house. All the cooking skills I had learnt from my mother stood to me now. Dr O'Brien loved the yeast bread I used to bake. He asked me to go to Tuam to look after his son's family who lived there.

I remember clearly going to Tuam. The family lived on Circular Road where the Post Office in Tuam is now situated and there were three children in the family to whom I taught Irish, among other things. The youngest, named Michael, was my special care. It is all pretty hazy now but I used to buy fish in a thriving fish market at the Square of Tuam and remember too going to Mass in the Cathedral. I liked Tuam very much. The people were very nice and sociable but I had no real acquaintance with anyone. It was there I received my first ever bouquet of flowers from a man who obviously liked me. I was a wild young thing that time and didn't take him seriously but getting the flowers was nice.

I stayed in Tuam for three or four months but two things shaped my leaving the place. First, my cousin Michael Wallace was killed at the front lines of World War I in France and that had a deep effect on me. He used to send me post cards from France, one of which I retain. The second reason for leaving concerned Mrs O'Brien's aversion to my teaching of Irish to her son. She was an English lady and had no time for the Irish language although her husband was thoroughly Irish. One day I was teaching the young lad and something struck him as very funny and he started to laugh. This was too much for his mother who took the book and threw it at her own son. The next morning when I got up, I had all my things packed up and took myself down to the Tuam Railway Station and set off for Knockavilla, County Tipperary to join my sister Julia who worked as a house-keeper for

Fr Matt Ryan, a great Irishman and follower of the nationalist movement. My time with that wonderful Irishman and PP in Knockavilla was to have a big bearing on my life. My sister Julia returned to Aran and I took over her job there. Julia incidentally lived to be a ripe old age like myself and died just after reaching her one hundredth year.

Chapter 9

Knockavilla, Cumann na mBan and The Tans

Fr Matthew Ryan, the PP in Knockavilla, was a Sinn Féin sympathiser and a true blue Irishman. He had been jailed himself during the Land League agitation long before this. So it was very fertile land for me to join Cumann na mBan and Tipperary was very much a rebel county, the county that produced Seán Treacy, Dan Breen and many other patriots. With the encouragement of the priest, my sister Julia, and his two nieces who lived in the house with their uncle, I joined the movement.

I joined because I felt it was a good cause. Our main aim at the time was to help out young men on the run. This was around 1918. In all, there were about 80 of us in that Tipperary based branch of the Cumann. We drilled in the same way as we saw the men do, copying their every movement. The men often gave us a lift to these drilling exercises, which were held at night in a big secluded field.

We prepared food for the men on the run and often took great risks in bringing food to them. We knew where to leave the food among the rocks and the heather or in a little house hidden in the bog. We had arranged these special meeting-places. If we had any spare money we gave it to them also. It was a tough time. There was little conversation if we happened to meet. It wasn't always the same men and there was seldom more than four or five of them together. The woods in question were known as the Bishop's woods. The names are hazy with me now but three surnames of the time were the Tierneys, O'Dwyers and O'Keeffes, all great Irishmen. Some died, many were arrested and it was a great privilege for us to help them in any way. All decent men, the finest this country produced. In all, I spent two years in Tipperary as a house-keeper for Fr Ryan. He often told us, 'When you talk to these men, tell them to call to my house if they wish me to hear their confessions.'

The Black and Tans were the scourge of Ireland at this time, creating terror every place they went. They were loathed by the people. Their uniform was a regular black suit with a yellow/orange stripe down along the side of the pants and also on the hems of the jacket. Hence, the name the Black and Tans. They came in big lorries, pillaging and looting, not caring who they shot. They shot into the air to create fear and some of their deeds were dastardly in the extreme. In Tipperary they shot a young lad in the back after telling him to run home. Around about this time too, Fr Griffin in Galway was taken from his house in Sea Road and murdered. I'm glad that men like Fr Griffin are remembered, with a road in Galway called after him and a football club in the city called Fr Griffins. Men and women who suffered and died for Ireland will always be remembered.

The Tans were very aware of our work in Tipperary but we were always one step ahead of them. When I returned to Aran after Knockavilla I remember the Black and Tans arriving by boat from Galway to the island. They had no lorries on the island, of course, but they had plenty of guns and ammunition. They were aware of my association with Cumann na mBan and raided our house in Oatquarter. Once they went to my cousin Martin Walsh's house while he was out fishing and stole all his money. In the evening when he returned, he was set upon, beaten up and taken to Galway by boat, dumped in jail and left there for a few weeks. Martin was known locally as a rebel. There were a lot like him in Aran at the time and the Tans never really got to grips with them.

One of their deeds is still remembered with hate for them and sadness for the poor young lad taken in the prime of his life. Laurence McDonagh was on his way to Mass one Sunday morning. They stopped him on his way and ordered him to go back home. So he set off and travelled on another road by the sea to get to Mass. Unfortunately, they met him and shot him dead. That was a most terrible time. We were glad to see the back end of them.

I still had the great desire to become a nurse. Just at this time the call came to start my Nursing training in the now defunct St Ultan's Children's Hospital in Ballsbridge, Dublin. This was the answer to all my dreams and I was on the next boat to Galway and by train to Dublin to answer the call. More adventures lay ahead and I was afraid of nothing at the time. The year was 1919.

Chapter 10

St Ultan's, the Bridewell and Mountjoy

In 1919, I arrived at St Ultan's Hospital to train as a nurse. The War of Independence was at its height and I continued to be a member of Cumann na mBan. It was a huge hospital and we lived and worked in the hospital itself. At that time too, a curfew was in place and people were not allowed out after 8 o'clock at night. Nurse training was then, I'm sure, quite different from today. At that time, during training and indeed after training, you were sent out to take care of specific cases and literally nurse people back to health.

While on one such nursing mission, I was taking care of a lady of English origin named Mrs Chevasse, after the birth of her child. Her husband, Claude Chevasse, was

French, a professor of languages, who worked from his own home and also travelled around from school to school. He was a well-known supporter of the Irish cause, then and subsequently, and was quite eccentric in dress, wearing kilts and always showing bare knees. He lived to be a ripe old age, I understand, and towards the end of his life was often seen in and around Galway while he lived beside Lough Corrib in Ross House. An incident happened in that house which I'll never forget.

I was reading a letter received from Aran from my cousin, Coleman Dirrane, informing me of activities on the island when I heard a knock on the door. I thought it was the postman returning with another letter. When I opened the door, a whole swarm of Black and Tans fell in on top of me like a plague of locusts. I ran to the kitchen to get the letter which contained some information of IRA movements. I managed to put the letter in the fire in time and this incensed the Tans. The officer in charge began to question me and I answered him *trí Ghaeilge ar fad* (through Irish all the time). He was furious and said many a person was shot dead for less. I answered him defiantly, 'I have only one life to give, but if I had a thousand lives to give, I'd give them for the same cause.' I told him to go ahead and shoot. He put the revolver down by his side and said, 'Get over there and put your coat on, you're under arrest.'

At that point I didn't care whether I was shot. I saw many a young man being shot after he was tortured. My life was worth very little compared to the lovely young men who were shot or hanged. I got my coat and went upstairs with one man holding on to my shoulder. They ransacked the house and arrested Mr Claude Chevasse and a lodger in the house at the time, Mr David O'Leary. All three of us were loaded into a lorry. They took us round the city and picked up other people at random before depositing us in the Bridewell. The Bridewell then was a terribly dirty place, a place for drunks and layabouts. I was left there for two days and two nights. Then I was transferred to Mountjoy Jail.

They took me out to the prison square where the lorry drivers were waiting. Some lorries were full of the prisoners. I refused to be put into one of the lorries and was forced to get in. Eventually, the lorries reached Mountjoy. While in the Bridewell I sang all the Irish songs I knew and danced away to my heart's content, making the officers furious. They were glad to get rid of me. Mountjoy was very clean compared to the Bridewell. There was no trial. Among the people in jail with me were Bridgy Brady and Mary McHale.

I continued to be troublesome in Mountjoy and went on hunger-strike there. Countess Markievicz was in Mountjoy at this time. The governor of the prison ordered the doctor to visit me. He ordered medication and a visit from a nurse daily. Two quarts of milk were sent to me every night. But I continued to be troublesome and never drank the milk but gave it to a little woman who was jailed for drinking too much and causing trouble and who was required to clean our cells. Looking back now I don't know how I survived. Eventually, the Mayor of Dublin sent in a good meal to all of us and I gave up the strike for that. Shortly after that I was released.

Once, Countess Markievicz came to my rescue when, after I had escorted Maud Gonne MacBride home late at night, I was pinned down by gunfire from a lorry-load of British troops. The Countess knew I was shocked and escorted me back to St Ultan's and insisted on my being placed in a special bed to ease my nerves and get some rest. There were many hair-raising encounters in the streets of Dublin then. It was an exciting, adventurous but extremely dangerous time. But thank God, I lived on.

Chapter 11

In Mountjoy Jail, one Monday morning...

In Mountjoy jail one Monday morning,
High upon the gallows tree,
Kevin Barry gave his young life,
For the cause of liberty;
Just a lad of eighteen summers,
And no one can deny;
As he walked to death that morning,
He proudly held his head on high.

These are the words of the song *Kevin Barry* which commemorates the student and Irish patriot of that name who was captured at Church Street, Dublin on September 20, 1920 and was hanged on November 1st of the same year.

With other members of Cumann na mBan I stood outside Mountjoy jail that Monday morning waiting to see the young lad being led to his death. We were outside the gate and saw him walk up with his guard. He looked so brave — no cries, no sound. He held his head high like he was going to be presented with a medal. We said the rosary together. When we heard the death bell toll, there was an eerie feeling abroad, then silence. We kept quiet in case we'd be arrested too. They hanged another rebel, Thomas Whelan, a week later and we were there again to say the rosary. It was a dreadful time but years afterwards, as I passed by Irish taverns in Boston or sat with Irish people at a sing-song or concert and heard *Kevin Barry* sung, I was proud to have been there that day. Nearly every Irish person I've ever met knows the song. I've sung it often myself.

The Civil War which followed the Treaty was dreadful. Brother against brother, relative against relative. I never supported the Michael Collins' side and was aghast when the Treaty was signed and accepted. I was even more aghast when guns were used to fire on the Four Courts and all hell broke loose. Was this what we had all fought for? I'm not saying Collins wasn't a fine man. I knew him well to see and for a time he lived near where I worked. Éamon de Valera was the man I admired then and always. I attended most of his meetings in Dublin and he loved Ireland with a passion. It is no surprise to me to see his grandson, Éamon Ó Cuív, a minister in Dáil Éireann today carrying on the family tradition and his grand-daughter, Síle, of the same name doing likewise.

All this time my nursing career continued and I was called by the doctors in St Ultan's to nurse here and there. In my training days I remember the excellent lectures and the care of Doctors Smith, Ryan, McGuire, Tennent and Barry. Once I travelled all the way North to Derry having got a call to go there from Dr Tennent to nurse a dying child. I can't remember the man's name whose child I nursed but he owned a clothing factory which employed 18 people. My last job as a nurse in Ireland was caring for the family of General Richard Mulcahy, known as Dick Mulcahy and a well-known figure in the first Dáil who became Minister for Defence. Life had returned to something like normality after all the troubles. The Mulcahys were lovely gentle folk and I had a lovely time there for over two years. Risteard, one of the children, later became one of Ireland's leading heart specialists. He was a grand little boy and I taught him a few words of Irish and he used to call me *'mo mhamaí féin'* (my own mammy). It's difficult to remember everything but I do remember the other Mulcahy children were Pádraig and Elizabeth.

From the St Francis Home I send best wishes to Risteard, the little boy I used to take on walks and remember his parents and family with great affection.

Once, while I was out walking with the Mulcahy children in Ballsbridge, I met my future husband Ned Dirrane. I don't remember whether it was by design or accident, but it was the first time I fancied him. We had grown up together in Inishmore and had often churned milk together in our youth. He attended school in Onaght while I was in Oatquarter school, in all a distance of six miles between us. But that distance was nothing to us. There were five boys in Ned's family, Ned, Patrick, John, Stephen and Michael and two girls Barbara and Mary. The next time I met Ned was in Boston. I was now thinking of emigrating and like so many Inishmore people before me, Boston was where I would go.

Chapter 12

America, Here I Come!

In 1927, I emigrated to America, Boston to be specific. Boston is the place where so many Inishmore people before me had gone and where so many of my relatives and friends lived. When I was growing up, nearly every household on the island lost one or two of their family to America. Their departure then was like a funeral. They would walk to Kilronan with a big suitcase, then on to Galway, after that to Dublin and the Globe Hotel, almost a station from America. Some of them never returned home. Worse still, some never lived to see America. Going away was easier when I left in 1927. I set sail from Cobh, or Queenstown as it was known then. Even at that stage we hadn't shed the English influences in so many areas! The ship I travelled on was a large and beautiful one—it may have been the

Franconia — which I certainly travelled on once. But everything on it was perfect. The voyage lasted seven days and despite the comfort and the luxury I was sick for most, if not all, of it.

The whole business of emigration from Aran and Ireland was not that traumatic an experience for me. I didn't mind leaving the native sod at all because quite a number of the volunteers from the troubled times had been deported or had emigrated and General Mulcahy (God rest his soul) helped me in every way, by giving me a lovely testimonial and vouching for me. I also wanted to continue my nursing career abroad, and besides, there were so many Aran people in Boston including my future husband, Ned Dirrane.

The ship, as I said, was very comfortable and the fare across cost me £12, a fair amount of money in those days but wouldn't get you very far today! On arrival in New York, all emigrants from Ireland were subjected to a very thorough medical examination, with special emphasis on eye-sight and general condition. If you failed this test you were sent to Ellis Island where you were kept in quarantine until you recovered. If you didn't improve, you were sent back home. Although I was sea-sick on the voyage and suffered ill-effects for some days afterwards I got through the medical with flying colours. That worry was over. My two cousins, Mary and Coleman Dirrane (blood relations from Inishmore, not relations of my future husband) were supposed to meet me at the docks but there was no sign of them. But I wasn't worried. I had made friends with many people on the voyage across, despite the sickness. Sure enough, in sailed Mary and Coleman and all three of us were soon on a train to Boston.

When I think of the journey across the broad Atlantic in that luxurious ship with a resident band on deck most of the time, I often think too of my first sea-trips across from Aran to Galway, a big venture then in my very young days. The first time I ever travelled to Galway by boat took three and a half hours and the fare was three shillings and six old pence, less than 20 pence in today's money. The name of the boat was the *Doorass* and it was piloted by Michael Folan. Everything and anything was on that boat. There was a pen down in the hold, downstairs, so to speak. You could have chickens, geese and ducks travelling alongside you. Nowadays, the very modern *Queen of Aran* travels from Galway to Aran in an hour and the Aer Arann plane which leaves from its own little airport at Indreabhán (Inverin) takes a mere six minutes to get you there. How things have changed!

My nursing career continued once I got to Boston and my first job was nursing for a Dr Emerson in a small general hospital in South Weymouth and this lasted for a year. A six-month stint followed in a much bigger medical hospital in Forest Hill in the south-west side of Boston. Then I nursed my cousin, Mary Dirrane, for a short time helping her recover from illness. For a time I felt the strains of over-working and was advised by my own doctor to take a complete break from nursing. This I did, taking a job as catering supervisor in a Boston Hotel. The name of the place was the Duncan Park Hotel and it prided itself on serving the best steaks in Boston.

When I came to Boston I joined the Galway Middle Club where young Irish people gathered every Saturday night for music, step-dancing and tea. You'd be sure to meet many Aran people there. Some I still remember, such as Jack and Tommy Folan from Kilronan, Michael and Mary Flaherty, Mary and Michael Hernon, George Dirrane and Nora Cooke from Kilmurvey. On those Saturday nights I often chatted with my two nephews, Joe and Patrick Gillan rambling on and on of old times. A céilí band which included Joe Dirrane, Gerry O'Brien and Tommy Shields provided high-class Irish music for us. We used to attend Mass at 2 a.m. on our way home from the dance. The Mass was held at that hour to accommodate the Irish workers. Life in America was not as easy as it is now.

I was to spend 39 years of my life in America.

Chapter 13

Wedding Bells in Boston

_E_ arly on in my days in Boston, I took a break from my nursing duties and spent a two-week vacation in Miami, Florida. It was like a different world. There was no crime there then. It was late in the year, after 'the Fall' as they called Autumn, and the sun shone brightly. Everything was so colourful and clean. The fruit was extraordinary — grapefruit, bananas _go leor_ (aplenty), plums and, believe it or not they cooked the loveliest oatmeal porridge in the Miami hotel I stayed in. You wouldn't get better in Aran. I travelled alone and really enjoyed my holiday where they spoilt me rotten. It was, I suppose, the first holiday I ever had.

Boston wasn't too much different from Dublin. In fact, I thought the streets of Dublin were far nicer. This was the time of the Depression in America and times were tough. There was gas but no electricity. If you needed light or heat you paid for the gas by inserting a nickel, dime or quarter. Similarly, if you wanted a cup of tea, you did likewise to boil the water. The job of a few of my Boston friends was to light the street lights at night. Edward Coyne, whose mother was from Aran and Bartley King from my own village of Oatquarter climbed the poles to light the gaslights. Bartley's nephew, Colman King, later became know as 'The Man of Aran'.

Quite a few men from the Connemara area worked for the gas company. Though the majority of them had little formal education, they became very skilful and talented and quite a number graduated to senior managerial status afterwards. We lived very simply. There were no mod cons like we have today. Many houses had to make do with candlelight. Believe it or not I was one of the first in the area in which I lived to purchase a fridge. Up until then, if you needed ice you'd have to go to the ice store situated in South Boston. People travelled from all around to collect ice. There was a slogan in vogue at the time: 'No money—no ice.' Buying ice was a bit of a novelty mainly for the big hotels or for the wealthy people. Most people made do without it.

The Irish worked hard to make ends meet. The Irish girls weren't afraid of hard work and many of them had to go down on their hands and knees to scrub floors. There was no marriage embargo on workers in the USA. A young girl could have two or three jobs and be married as well. Some of the wealthy Jewish people were very suspicious of the young girls they hired who had just come over from Ireland. They often left money lying around in containers to tempt them and test their honesty. But we got wise to the gambit and the Irish girls were advised to be on their guard. I recall looking after a sick little boy, both of whose parents were Jewish. As well as nursing him, part of my duty was to keep his room tidy. On the telephone seat was a $10 bill and I drew it to the notice of the lady of the house straight away. But I was annoyed and said, 'Just because I am Irish doesn't mean I am dishonest. Never again do that to any Irish girl. They come over here, they work very hard for their living and they deserve more respect.' I also asked her to pass on the message to her Jewish friends.

When I went to Boston first I lived in Dorchester. It was a great Irish neighbourhood then but like everywhere else now, you have every colour and creed. The people from Aran and Galway kept in close contact with one another. Shortly after I went to Boston, I met Ned Dirrane again, my future husband. This time it was at his aunt's house, that of Mary Walsh who was married to my cousin Bartley. I was going out with Ned for a few years prior to our marriage. We used to meet about once a fortnight, sometimes more often than that, work schedules permitting.

Our marriage took place in the month of November 1932 in St Thomas Aquinas Church in Jamaica Plains, Boston. I wore a long pink dress with a big velvet satin sash. The hat was huge and dressed in white and pink. My bouquet was made up of lilies. The congregation or attendance at the ceremony was small but we had a great reception in my cousin Kate Bowe's house in Jamaica Plains. Our wedding took place in the afternoon and the dinner was over by 7 p.m. Nobody travelled from Aran or Ireland for the occasion. Mary Bowe was my bridesmaid and John Flaherty was Ned's best man, both Aran people. Mary's dress was a long pink one. I bought the material and made the dresses having always been good at dressmaking, knitting and crochet. In fact, just today as I talk, I knitted a pink bonnet which I hope to present to a friend for their new-born child.

We were both in our thirties when we got married. We went to live in Third Street, South Boston, renting an apartment from a Connemara man named John Folan. All we had was a kitchen, a bedroom and small dining area, for which we paid him 70 cents per week. We made many friends in Third Street. Barbara Conneely from Inishmore was a near neighbour. The Berrys, John and Mary, lived closeby also. Mary was from Killeany and John from Connemara and there were cousins *go leor* (aplenty) living in the vicinity. We tended to take care of each other in so many ways.

A few days after our wedding, I started nursing in Forest Hill Hospital in Jamaica Plains while Ned worked in a local wool store. Bags of wool used to come in from the West and his job was to separate the good wool from the bad. The fleeces used to get extremely hard after the long journey as they were very tightly packed. He worked hard and had long hours starting at 8 a.m. and was paid 22 cents per hour, which improved, in time, to $1 per hour. I worked long and hard too, doing much overtime and being paid a good rate per hour. It was difficult to make ends meet but we got by, leading a very simple but happy life. Things weren't to get better until Franklin D. Roosevelt came into power.

Chapter 14

Cardinal Cushing, Irishman through and through

My career in America was interesting, varied and full of adventure. I remained very close to God always, remembering my upbringing at home in Aran and always fervent in my devotion to Our Lady. After Ned and I got married we had frequent visits to our apartment from Fr Connolly, Fr Beatty and Fr Kearns. I have always been a staunch Catholic and proud of my religion. Catholic churches were dotted everywhere in Boston. I can still recall their names and locations: St Monica's of the Rosary, St Vincent's, St Peter and Paul's and my own special favourite, The Gate of Heaven (which I always thought was a lovely name for a church).

I remember once leaving my rosary beads after me in the church. A few days later Fr Kearns gave the beads back to me. When I enquired how he knew they were mine he said, 'Sure you never leave them out of your hands Bridget.' I still have a bead or two from those rosary beads and I still keep rosary beads in my hands always. I've worn out a fair number of them in my lifetime!

I was asked by one of the priests in 'The Gate of Heaven' church to make a special long robe for the statue of the Blessed Virgin. Using white satin I made it in two days. The train was made in such a way that it would take five or six children to carry it at the local processions. It was much admired and I often wonder if it lasted long in my favourite church.

I knew Cardinal Cushing well, an Irishman through and through. He was very close to the Kennedy family and did any amount of good work for the Boston Irish. He helped to get employment for so many of them. He was tall, strong and sturdy, with a very determined voice. I received many invitations from him to attend special Masses and functions. His rosary and benediction, which were usually held in Milton, Massachusetts in East Boston used to attract thousands of people. He liked to get things done and helped to renovate the Carney Catholic Hospital in Boston among many other achievements. I spent four weeks recuperating there after a serious road accident in which I received a fractured skull, torn ligaments and muscles. The accident happened between High St and Dorchester St in South Boston. As I crossed the road, in a hurry (as usual), I was struck by a passing car. It was all my own fault. I was lucky to survive but I do believe in 'mind over matter'. The poor man who ran into me was in an awful way. He called to see me in hospital and gave me $100 which helped to pay my medical bills.

I was glad that Cardinal Cushing was the church dignitary chosen to bless the Galway Cathedral on its official opening day in the '60s because he put a lot of money into its construction, helped, of course, by the many Boston-Galway people. Boston recognised the contribution Galway people made to their city over the years.

Ned and myself hadn't that much time together in married life. We were married for eight years when God called him away through heart failure. I got through the trauma, remembering how well my own mother coped when her husband (Dad) died when I was seven or eight years old in Aran. I was the youngest of eight and she reared us so well, considering that she was on her own for most of us. If she could do it, surely I could too. I never had any children of my own but that was God's will and I accepted my lot. I was, however, associated with children all my life through nursing and care and then, of course, there were the children of so many of my cousins who regarded me as a mother. Risteárd

Aran, the island where Bridget was born. (By kind permission of Colman Doyle)

Mending the nets. From left to right: Joe Gillan (brother), Patrick Gillan (cousin and neighbour), Margaret (Bridget's mother) and John Cremins (neighbour).

Family and friends. From Left to Right: Bartley Faherty, John Gillan (brother), Margaret Anne (sister), Pat Flaherty, Bridget and Joe (brother) (1917).

Bridget's sister Julia in her younger days. Julia lived to be 100.

'My little Bundleen' (bundle). Risteard Mulcahy as a youngster.

Bridget Dirrane's first husband, Edward.

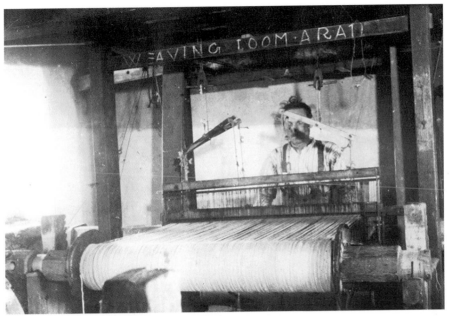

Joe Gillan (brother) at the loom.

Bridget Dirrane
(aged 50).

CERTIFICATE
OF
APPRECIATION

AWARDED TO

BRIDGET DIRRANE

PLANT NURSE—MC CULLOCH MFG. CO.

IN RECOGNITION OF

HER

EFFORTS AND SUCCESS

IN

PREVENTING

LOST TIME ACCIDENTS

AUGUST 4, 1943

VICE-PRESIDENT

Certificate of Appreciation,
Boston, 1943.

Continuing the family
tradition of weaving
(1957).

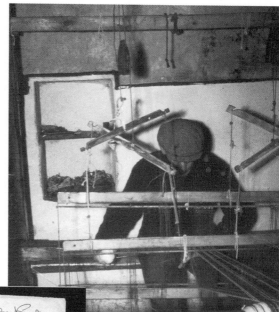

Correspondence from
Jacqueline Kennedy to
Bridget.

Bridget and her second husband Pat outside Cliff Edge Cottage.

Sewing potatoes in Aran. (By kind permission of Colman Doyle)

Bridget and her
second husband
Pat, celebrating
Thanksgiving
Day in Aran, a
custom which
Bridget took
back with her
from the States.

Bridget's dog 'Captain' who was a
great favourite.

Cliff Edge Cottage in Oatquarter, very much the creation of Bridget.

Bridget dancing a Jig at
the age of 90 plus!

Music was part of the
Gillan tradition. Bridget
playing her accordion.

Bridget on her return to Aran by Aer Arann.

The statue erected by Bridget in 1994 at the well of the Four Beautiful Saints.

United States Senate

WASHINGTON, DC 20510

October 21, 1994

Ms. Bridget Dirrane
Cliff Edge Cottage Oat Quarter
Irishmore Aran Islands
County Galway
Ireland

Dear Bridget:

I am delighted to add my congratulations to those of your many friends and family on the occasion of your one-hundredth birthday on November 15th.

You have been granted a long and productive life, and I greatly admire your tremendous spirit. My warmest wishes are with you and your family on this special day.

With warm regards,

Sincerely,

Edward M. Kennedy

Edward M. Kennedy

Birthday Greetings from Edward!

Bridget with Jean Kennedy-Smith at
St Francis' Home in Newcastle, Galway.

Bridget outside the house in which she was born.
This photo was taken in 1997.

Bridget with her step-grandchildren: Michael, Ciarán and Timmy

Dusk approaches on Aran. (By kind permission of Colman Doyle)

Mulcahy was one such child who regarded me as a parent. My step-grandchildren who live in Aran are special pets of mine.

My nursing days continued in Boston and after my stay in Forest Hill, South Weymouth, I worked in a Jewish hospital and then worked as a District or Public Health Nurse for some time. You'd be called to another case as soon as you'd be finished with one patient. Arising from this I started my career with the American military in an accidental way. I nursed a lady called Mrs McCullagh, whose husband Albert, was owner and manager of the Ammunition Factory nearby. It was wartime now in the US and the whole country wanted to see the Allies win the war. Unfortunately, Mrs McCullagh died of cancer but my career changed course at this stage as a direct result of meeting the McCullagh family.

Chapter 15

From Boston to Mississippi and Alabama

The day Mrs McCullagh died, her daughter noticed me polishing my shoes in preparation for leaving. 'Where are you going, Bridget?' she asked.

'That depends on my next call,' I replied.

'Go down to see Dad first,' she said. 'I know he has something to say to you.'

My first reaction was one of fear. What on earth had I done wrong? There and then Mr McCullagh offered me a job as plant nurse in his munitions factory. I held this job for two years at the beginning of World War II.

My main job was to look after injuries or pains and aches sustained at work in a factory of over 80 employees. Much wire, tin and glass was used. The employees' jobs were dangerous and quite a number of them were unskilled. Injuries to fingers were inevitable. Girls had to be quite careful about tying up their hair. One of my first tasks was to advise on safety precautions. Back injuries from lifting heavy loads were frequent. Despite the dangers and the carelessness at times, the inevitable injuries were treatable and most injuries healed soon enough. All the machinery in the plant was run by oil which was stored in large tanks outside the building. Smaller drums were used to pour oil into the machines. From early days, I took a general interest in the plant and ensured the machinery was always well oiled.

I took a bigger interest in the factory floor and before long was able for any kind of work associated with the plant. I remember early on coming across 36 boxes of faulty triggers attached to guns and in two months had them all repaired. When you come from Aran you need to be able to tackle anything! I became a good judge of the suitability of iron for making guns. The iron had to be light and long for gun barrels. By the time I left that plant I was as good a mechanic as I was a nurse and if anything went wrong with the machinery day or night the word went out, 'Send for Bridget'.

We made bombs or rather containers for bombs on site too. It was vital that the first hole drilled in the metal plate was properly done. Everything fitted into place after that. We did not feel guilty making all these for use in the war, although I must say I often said three Hail Marys as I helped to make them, hoping some lives and souls would be saved. America was at war and munitions factories were producing guns, ammunition and bombs for the US forces fighting overseas. For my work in that plant I was paid $20 a week. Hours were from 8 a.m. to 7 p.m. and I was happy to move on.

Following on from that, on a recommendation from Mr McCullagh, I found myself working for the Military Airforce and was sent on a mission to take care of American soldiers down in Mississippi near the Gulf of Mexico. It was at one of the largest bomber bases in the US. It was my duty to care for and prescribe medication for the sick. Believe it or not I drilled the same as I did many years before with Cumann na mBan. Mississippi was a beautifully green place and I'd never have left it, if I had any of my own living nearby. The people I encountered there were all strangers to me. There was a very unusual climate there—on dry, balmy days, if you hung clothes out to dry, they'd never dry. But on wettish damp days your clothes would dry no bother. Don't ask me how!

I have other memories from my time in Mississippi. When travelling to the airbase from Boston I passed the White House in Washington DC for the first time. And when I reached green Biloxi in Mississippi I was reminded of old times in Oatquarter when my brother John would line a few of us up every day to spell three words—Mississippi,

Constantinople and Missouri. They were strange names to us then and little did I know I would be working in Mississippi— in Keesler Field, Biloxi to be exact. While there, I often went to Alabama to visit some Irish priests in the area. Alabama was another lovely place with flowers everywhere. One day, while walking down the street with a fur coat on me, one of the priests stopped me and said, 'Wouldn't you look lovely walking over to Kilronan in that!' You'd meet Irish people everywhere. I knew four priests in Alabama— two Fr Murphys, Fr O'Donoghue and Fr Fitzgerald—you can't get names more Irish than that! There were quite a few Roman Catholic soldiers in Keesler Field and every Tuesday I used to make pancakes for them after Mass or rosary. I met all creeds and colours in my time in the States. On my birthday I was presented with a beautiful purse by some of my friends.

And so life continued in America as World War II drew to a close.

Chapter 16

'Nearly everybody in Boston comes from Galway'

President John F. Kennedy visited Galway in June 1963.
His visit was received with scenes of wild enthusiasm
and, in his speech at Eyre Square, on June 29, 1963
before he received the Freedom of Galway City from the
Mayor of Galway Alderman Paddy Ryan, this is what he said:

'Mr Mayor, members of the City Council, Prime Minister,
Ambassadors.

If the day was clear enough and if you went down to the
bay and you looked west and your sight was good enough you
would see Boston, Massachusetts. And if you did, you would
see down working on the docks there the O'Dohertys, Flahertys
and Ryans and cousins of yours who have gone to Boston and
made good. I wonder if you could, perhaps, let me know how

many of you here have relatives in America, whom you'd admit to? If you would, hold up your hands.

I don't know what it is about you that causes me to think that nearly everybody in Boston comes from Galway. They are not shy about it, at all. I want to express as we are about to leave here to tell you in this country how much this visit has meant.

It is strange that so many years could pass and so many generations pass and still some of us who came on this trip could come home here to Ireland and feel ourselves at home and not feel ourselves in a strange country but feel ourselves among neighbours even though we are separated by generations, by time and by thousands of miles.

So you have made all of us. You send us home covered with gifts which we can barely carry but most of all, most of all, you send us home with warmest memories of you and your country.

So I must say that although other days be not so bright as we look towards the future, that the brightest days will continue to be those on which we visited you here in Ireland. If you ever come to America, come to Washington and tell them if they wonder who you are at the gate that you come from Galway. The word will be out, and when you do, it will be 'Céad Míle Fáilte', which means in Gaelic 'A Hundred Thousand Welcomes'. (*Extract courtesy of The Mantle, Galway Diocesan Magazine 1963 entitled Irish Visit.*)

I admired the Kennedys greatly, especially John F. Kennedy who became President of the USA. I valued every hair on his head and was lucky to be in Boston for the Kennedy era and proud to have canvassed for him door to door, at shopping malls in the South Boston area. He was a great Irishman and a man to be proud of. I was always well received and at times when I knocked at doors, it was like as if I was at home in Aran or Connemara. Practically every home had Irish connections, the majority of them coming from the west.

Boston really supported the Kennedys politically and a fine team of helpers and canvassers got involved in JFK's Presidential campaign. I sent him a special good luck and Mass card wishing himself and his family every success in his venture and I still have his letter of acknowledgement in my possession. At the same time my brother George back home in Aran (the man who knew Sinéad de Valera) had become a huge supporter of John F. Kennedy too and corresponded with the future President. Most of all I worked for and respected JFK because of his strong Irish roots and the pride he brought to all Irish Catholics working in the States that, at last, we would have a Catholic of Irish blood as President. It was a great time to be Irish and a Catholic, the day he was elected. His visit to Ireland and his speech in Galway let everybody know how much he thought of Ireland and Galway.

His mother, Rose Kennedy, was a wonderful person. If ever there was a real lady she was one. She suffered many troubles in her life and bore them all with a dignity which was an example to us all. She lived to a great age like myself, *buíochas le Dia* (thanks be to God). One hundred and four I do believe. Her great faith in God kept her going through all the ordeals.

The Kennedys do not forget either—even a humble person like myself who canvassed for JFK almost 40 years ago. Jean Kennedy-Smith, sister of JFK visited me in St Francis' Home, Galway recently and we were photographed together. She also visited me in my home—Cliff Edge Cottage in Oatquarter. One day, a young man knocked on my door. With a distinct American accent he asked, 'Is this Bridget Dirrane's house?' When I answered yes he continued, 'My name is William Kennedy-Smith. My Mom, Jean Kennedy-Smith, will be here shortly. She is on her way by bicycle.' I couldn't believe my ears! She arrived shortly afterwards and yes, it was the American Ambassador to Ireland. The youngest of the Kennedy clan, Teddy, also visited me in Aran with his son. When he was leaving I said to him, 'Don't forget to take care of the Kennedys,' to which he replied, 'I sure will'. On the occasion of his visit to Aran, he dined at *Tigh Stiofáin* (The House of Stephen) owned by my son-in-law Stiofán Dirrane.

I was coming to the end of my years in the States. After the war I continued nursing around the States. I had learnt to drive at this stage and drove my own Bel-Air Chevy for ten years prior to coming home. Boston was now so much different from the Boston of the '30s and the Depression. There was plenty of money and plenty of work and plenty of everything. Wealth and riches abounded. It was a different place altogether and yet despite the affluence, even in the best of times there was sadness. And in the worst of times when people used to be fed a cup of soup and one meatball at the special feeding stations for the poor, there often was a ray of hope and much basic friendship. I had now retired from nursing and was living with my nephew and his family. It was time to go home to Aran to retire for good. The children Robert and Joey cried when I left for home because I took them everywhere with me. Years afterwards when I returned on a visit Joey — a big man then — put his two arms around me and lifted me off the ground with delight. And so to Aran and home.

Chapter 17

Summers

I had come to the end of my days in the States. It was time to head home to Aran. During my 39 years in the States, I had never lost touch with home. South Boston was an extension of Inishmore in a way! Twice during my time living in the States I had returned home and on both occasions I visited Lourdes. My devotion to Our Lady never wavered through my life. I'll never forget the cool feeling on being dropped into the baths in Lourdes. I don't think I'd survive it today though I'd love to return there, for it is a special place. On that first visit to Lourdes I was accompanied by my sister Margaret and my niece Julia. Knock is another favourite place which I have visited several times. I'll make a trip to Knock again hopefully!

Fate was kind to me in allowing me to return to the 'ould sod' hale and hearty in 1966. I was 72 years old and delighted to be *sa bhaile* (at home) among family, neighbours and friends. For me it was a new beginning and the closing of an old file, attached to which was so much struggle, strife and hardship, but also one which carried much adventure and excitement.

Aran too had changed, much of it for the better. It was no longer the simple, often isolated place it was in my young days, where we all ran wild and free. Tourism had opened Aran to the world and the Aran islands had become a popular visiting place, with the local population benefiting considerably from the Tourism boom. B & B's had began to boom creating much work on the islands. It's a trend that has grown and grown over the years. It has, of course, brought many compensations but hopefully will not kill Aran's unique culture, traditions and way of life.

When I returned even the weather seemed to have changed. Or is it just that we tend to remember sunny days and black out the wet, miserable ones that must have been there too? I don't honestly think so. Where, oh where, have all the beautiful summers of long ago gone to? I remember how the summer started in early April with the cuckoo's call and, at times, went straight into and through September long after the cuckoo had departed. During those long, hot summers drinking water was scarce. The well in Inishmore which kept everyone supplied with water when all the others had dried up was known as the Big Well and was situated just opposite our house in Oatquarter. Thousands of buckets of water were drawn from that well and even in the hottest of droughts it was never known to have run dry.

Thunder and lightning outbreaks, or as the Yanks would call it, 'a storm' were much more striking then than today. It was common enough to have several such storms in a month. It was big news among the Aran folk in Boston when we heard that Michael Conneely's house in Shrawn had been struck and damaged by lightning. You can imagine also the great shock waves in the whole island when a horse in the Mainistir area was struck dead by lightning. The horse was a very valued animal in Aran in those days. Unfortunately, the horse is fast leaving Irish country life, his place having been taken by machinery such as tractors. Horses were so full of nature. They knew their master, responded to his call and were very much part of almost every house then.

Likewise, the good old donkey has almost disappeared from Irish life. How often do you see a donkey and cart today unless outside some pub or other reminding us of a past rapidly receding? In Aran today though, there are plenty of sidecars whisking tourists from one end of the island to the other, a distance of seven or eight miles. It was no bother to Aran people to walk it in the past and signs on them, many of them lived a fit and healthy life afterwards.

In my youth, nearly every village on the island had a wee shop, although it never seemed wee to us! Our local shop belonged to my aunt, Mary Dirrane, and I remember with great affection running up and down to the shop buying 'bull's eyes' and 'peggy's legs'. Another nice shop at the edge of our village was called *Siopa Gilbert* (Gilbert's Shop). It, alas, like so many others, is no more. He always had fresh groceries and specialised in the sale of bran and oatmeal for baking. It's a pity that the coming of supermarkets has put so many groceries and small shops out of business.

Much of our young days were spent running in the fields around Dun Aengus, which is situated in the most westerly point of our island—as John F. Kennedy said, 'Next stop America!' Once, when I was 15 years old, one of my cousins threatened to throw me off the cliff edge near Dun Aengus and dragged me there. I was scared to death and eventually got away. I don't think he intended doing it, but he was good at fooling! If our respective parents knew we were within a mile of those cliffs we'd have been locked up for weeks.

And so I was back in the Aran I loved for the final chapter of a long life.

Chapter 18

Never a cross word between us…

Back in Aran after all my wandering I found myself living with my brother-in-law, Pat Dirrane, in his house at Oatquarter. Pat was no stranger to me. Like his brother Ned, we had grown up together in Inishmore as one big, happy family and there was a *céad míle fáilte* (a hundred thousand welcomes) in that house for me. He, like myself, had married before and his wife Sarah O'Toole from Bongoola had died at a young age leaving him to rear three sons: Stephen, Johnny and Coleman. At this stage—1966—all three were living abroad, Stephen in USA and John and Coleman across the water in England.

I was now in my early seventies, Pat in his sixties. We had always been great friends. So we both decided it was best to get married to protect our good name, maintain respect in our community and show good example. As I say this, it sounds cold and very proper. To put it simply, we got on well and it was the natural thing to do and the decision is one neither of us ever regretted. Next morning I was up to our PP, Fr McNamara to tell him of our decision and ask him to help arrange a quiet wedding and marriage ceremony for us. He was absolutely supportive, contacted the Bishop of Galway, Most Rev. Dr Browne and arranged for us to be married in St Joseph's Church in Galway on April 27, 1966. It was a very private affair and a closely guarded secret. Nobody in Aran knew what we intended doing and we both wanted it that way. I bought a nice navy outfit in Ryan's of Galway and Pat purchased a new suit too.

The wedding was a very simple affair, just four of us present, my sister-in-law Celia who acted as bridesmaid and my brother Joe who was Pat's best man. After dinner in Galway we headed back for Aran. It is very unusual to marry two brothers. They were so different in many ways. Pat was a lovely man, so humorous and full of fun and loved dancing. When I think back now and remember the nights in Cliff Edge Cottage—our home—when we danced the night away together, it brings a tear to my eye. Any funny remark I'd make he'd laugh aloud and would remind me again of it a few days later. We must have been six months married before anyone in Inishmore knew about it. We got on like a house on fire. There was never a cross word between us and we went everywhere together.

We were both staunch Catholics and said the rosary each night together. I always trusted in the Lord and even though my married life was short with both Ned and Pat, I feel a better woman today for having known and married them. Unfortunately Pat's poor health gave me quite a lot of concern especially in his latter years. He survived a number of mild strokes before a severe stroke finally brought an end to his suffering. But he was never demanding and I nursed him right up to the end. He died peacefully on Ash Wednesday, 1990, as we recited the rosary at the bedside. I was very lonely then and am lonely for him still. He is buried in the family plot in Killeany graveyard and I had a nice headstone placed on his grave. When my time comes that's where I'll be buried too.

I bonded my two wedding rings together as a token of my love for the two Dirrane brothers Ned and Pat and they travel with me everywhere I go. When I die I'm bequeathing the bonded rings to my step-son Coleman who returned from England to live with Pat and myself in Cliff Edge Cottage. I'll never forget the warmth of his embrace when he put his two arms around me and said I belonged to his family too. It was the reassurance I needed. From that day to this we never separated. There was plenty of everything in that house. Most of all there was love.

Chapter 19

We had simple fun which cost little

The Aran I returned to in 1966 was much different from the one I left in the late '20s. I took great pride in the renovation of Cliff Edge Cottage almost from the time I started to live there—and often did the reconstruction myself. One of my first observations was noticing how a pool of water gathered outside the main doorstep on a wet day. So I bought cement, got some sand from Kilmurvey and reset the doorstep myself. I didn't need any man to mix or set the concrete for me. In fact, years afterwards when further reconstruction was necessary, it was almost impossible to break the concrete I had set!

Coleman and I also built a solid wall to replace the old timber partition separating the dining-room from the kitchen.

Again, Coleman and I raised the roof, put down new floors and built two larger rooms upstairs. It was no bother to me at all to work on the roof at 73 years of age, and I helped to slate the roof and certainly oversaw it all. That work is still to be seen in Oatquarter and hopefully will stand the passage of time. I was involved in all aspects of the reconstruction, even to the construction of a new fireplace in the dining-room. Pat often went off for a walk leaving me to work away on a job. Afterwards, I took great pleasure in planting all the trees and flowers which surround the cottage.

The greatest joy of all for me was to be embraced into the warmth of a young family and help in the rearing of Timmy, Michael and Ciarán, the three darling children of Coleman and Margaret. All three were born in the Regional Hospital in Galway before returning home to Aran, as is the custom now. That young family brought life to the home and I regarded them as my own and love them all dearly.

Life in Aran, as I said, had changed a lot but was not as changed as it is now. Electricity, running water and Aer Arann had still to come but weren't far away. When I left, the only transport was by bicycle or foot. When I returned there were a few automobiles and vans on the island. The provision of electricity and running water was tremendous for the island. I couldn't help remembering the kerosene lamps of my youth. I remember, in particular, one farmer's wife who lived nearby (all of whose people are dead now) who had a little font, like the well of my cupped hand, and they used to put a wick into the font, full of oil which they had got from sea fish. It was difficult enough to get that kind of oil and you'd only get a jar-full from a whole lot of fish.

'Hunting' for food would regularly take place at night when oil was scarce and no candles were available for light. A man would be lowered in the pitch black of night down to the ledges of the cliff face to sit and wait for the puffins. He might capture 30 a night, killing them by twisting their necks. They were lovely to eat and were like little chickens, and we used to boil them in pots. I used to love rock birds myself. You'd have to wait until they fell asleep to catch them in the rocks.

Before the light came we used gas in Aran, something I had got quite used to in the States many years earlier. You could say I saw the coming of electricity twice in my life. And when I think of the electrical heat such as storage heaters, I couldn't help remembering the turf fires of old, turf we imported from Connemara, or the great use we made of driftwood found regularly on the shore, or during the long hot summers, the dried cow droppings which made for a good fire. Very often those cow droppings were dried out and preserved and, when seasoned, would light like paper and help start the fire!

Another great change was in the design of the houses and the changing dress styles. In the old days, the family home was a standard design of a kitchen and two bedrooms with no running water or toilet. It was quite common for the thatch to leak during a steady downpour and for the dampness to ooze down the walls. We used to wear red flannel dresses and costumes while the older folk all wore Aran shawls. You wouldn't see too many Aran women wearing shawls today. Not uncommon then was to see young men wearing the white sleeveless *bréidín* (hand-woven woollen material) which were very attractive in their own right but are seldom worn today.

Aer Arann, when it came, was a fantastic boost to the islands and I was one of the first Aran people to travel to the islands by plane. I remember travelling by boat into Galway and it was arranged that I return by plane in the company of Government representatives, Mr Michael Woods and Mrs Máire Geoghegan-Quinn, on the inaugural flight. I remember presenting Mr Hayden, the pilot, with a dozen crystal glasses and a framed scene of Aran. Another great pilot was Mr Wallace who once brought us to Shannon Airport safely after a scary fog-bound flight. The crews on these planes were and are so courteous and I've travelled to and from Aran by plane umpteen times.

Nowadays fun and games are more organised and youngsters spend much time watching videos and television. There were no big sports days in Aran in our day but we had plenty of fun. We youngsters got great enjoyment out of simple things which cost little or nothing. The most popular game in my youth was 'Rucco', something like hurling or camogie today. We cut the sticks from trees or large bushes to form our kind of hurleys and we played the game with a sponge ball in Kilmurvey. Handball up against the gables of the houses was very popular also.

We ran at night in the moonlight and the first youngster to fall into the sandpit in Kilmurvey was the winner. My cousin Martin Walsh and my brother Joe were excellent at rock-throwing, another popular sport which was a real test of strength. The way the rock was held in the palm of the hand was crucial. Football too was very popular. We made our own footballs from balls of yarn or old clothes. My mother (God rest her) was a great card-player at either Twenty-five or Forty-five. In winter, the locals used to gather in different houses to play for a boxty cake (a cake made from potatoes and flour). The losers had to make the cake and present it to the winners. The cake wasn't everybody's cup of tea but such was the custom! Simple fun and costing little. *Sin mar a bhí sé in Árainn fadó* (that's the way it was in Aran years ago).

Chapter 20

Everybody seems to be rushing to the graveyard

I don't like to preach but as this is the final chapter you'll spare me, if in the wisdom of old age, I hand on a few words of advice.

I'm no stranger to the media especially over the past few years but this book is what I'm leaving behind me and I hope, *le cúnamh Dé* (with God's help) to live to see it launched.

To adults and parents I say, always try a little kindness. Think positively, act swiftly and do your best to share your talents. To the youth of Ireland I say stick to your books and take advantage of the great educational opportunities available to you, always respect your parents for our country needs fine, educated people to carry on the good work of previous generations. Please don't move too far away from the Lord. For as the song says, miracles do happen. Always be yourselves and try not to follow the crowd. Give yourself enough room to develop. But I'm preaching too much!

Sometimes I'm asked what is the recipe for living a long life. It seems to run in the genes. One of my sisters, Julia, lived to be 100 years of age but my sister, Mary, died at 21 years of age. So where is the logic in that?! However, I do believe that people who live beside the sea are much healthier than people from inland. Diet also plays a big factor. Green vegetables are a must. Pastries and fries are deadly. I always loved the traditional bacon and cabbage dish but beware of too much salt in the bacon. Brown wholemeal bread has always been my favourite and we need plenty of fibre in our diet. I still love fruit. Many people today waste time and money going on needless diets whereas if they adhered to a consistent diet of vegetable, fruit and fish they'd be better, fitter and more contented people.

Exercise is terribly important too. We seldom walk anywhere anymore and must use the motor car even to do a simple message. I often walked from Bongoola to the other side of Aran, the whole length of Inishmore and it didn't bother me one whit. Finally, if you want to have some quality of life, stress must be controlled. When I was a young *cailín* (girl) there was a different kind of stress out there. Yes, we had hard times but we shared and related better. Girls related to girls, boys to boys, women to women and I remember the men lining up outside the church before and after Mass on Sunday to talk and chat for ages. You never passed a person on the road without stopping for a wee chat unless it was pouring rain and the quick hello sufficed. Today, unfortunately, people don't have the time to bid each other the time of day. Everybody seems to be rushing to the graveyard!

Now that I have found a final resting place in St Francis Home, Newcastle, Galway after a long adventurous, exciting and, at times, arduous life I have lashings of time to dwell on the past and the present. Everybody else here is a youngster compared to me even though it is a home for the elderly. I'm confined to a wheelchair mostly, but I can still walk a wee bit and do so every day. The most important item on my agenda now is to make my peace with God. All my old friends and neighbours both in Aran and the US are dead and gone and there is only myself left to write the story. I cherish life still and I firmly believe nobody should want to die. I'd like to live a few more years. Still, every day is a bonus and my life is in the good Lord's hands.

I still have a few things to do! I hope to live for the launch of this book and the excitement of it all doesn't bother me. If I'm well enough and if I'm invited I'll do my best to accommodate the media. I hope the book will get across the message to the elderly that anything is possible even at 103. I want to return to Aran as often as possible before the final journey home. I want to see my step-grandchildren, Timmy, Michael and Ciarán at school in Oatquarter once again. I'd like to have another visit from Jean Kennedy-Smith. Most of all I want to see peace in our country for all time. A permanent peace.

You may ask what will I leave behind me when I go for good? It won't be riches. What I will leave is the sunshine to the flowers, honey to the bees, the moon above in the heavens for all those in love and my beloved Aran Islands to the seas.

Agus sin a bhfuil (That's it).